Unexpectedly

A Collection of Poems

Unexpectedly

Maithree Wickramasinghe

EBURY
PRESS

An imprint of Penguin Random House

EBURY PRESS

Ebury Press is an imprint of the Penguin Random House group of companies
whose addresses can be found at global.penguinrandomhouse.com

Published by Penguin Random House India Pvt. Ltd
4th Floor, Capital Tower 1, MG Road,
Gurugram 122 002, Haryana, India

Penguin
Random House
India

First published in Ebury Press by Penguin Random House India 2025

Copyright © Maithree Wickramasinghe 2025

Photograph of Maithree Wickramasinghe by Heshani Sothiraj Eddleston

ISBN 9780143474401

Typeset in Papyrus by Manipal Technologies Limited, Manipal
Printed at Replika Press Pvt. Ltd, India

www.penguin.co.in

MIX
Paper | Supporting
responsible forestry
FSC™ C016779

For RW

My sincere thanks to
Nadira, Sharni, Ralph, Kan, Milee, Saloni, Ram,
Mariam, Sunela, Rangita, Harshi, Kirthi, Kumi, Totsy, Amalee

Contents

Part One: Unexpectedly

Part Two: In Extremis

Part One

Unexpectedly

'These poems have their origins in the poet's imagination
of the exquisite in the everyday, the mysteries of the
metaphysical; chafing socio-political realities and experiences
of disease, adversity, and impending death, written essentially
as private reflections.'

Blood Orange

These days
there is a fingernail
scraping and scraping
the skin of our minds—
with a simple flick
of a fingernail—
scraping and scraping
with a tenacity
that can split the rind
to swell blood orange
under a fingernail—
scraping and scraping
to flip us over
the flange of fury
with a fingernail—
scraping and scraping
to enflame us
into Molotov cocktails
with a trifling fingernail.

Colourings

Some people colour me Blue in blood;
while others assume a partisan Green—
especially if cut wide open;
still others ascribe an academic White
in candlelight;
those who don't know me
smear a bright Pink stereotype
but I,
I paint myself a feminist Purple.
Yet horse sense makes me think that blood is Red
but who knows what colour blood
once you are dead.

Hot War in the Middle East

In the Middle East
hot war ruptures,
from time to time—

a rash of boiling water bubbles.

Scalded hands on either side
imploring their private god
to maim and mutilate
to slay and annihilate
to massacre and exterminate
to bomb and bombard
to displace and demolish
the neighbourhood enemy
on the other side.

In other worlds,

dinner table colloquies
track historical injuries
trace territorial ancestries
dispute digital tallies
defend indefensible atrocities
affirm tribal mentalities
ascend moral precipices—

Cont.

raving like Bulbul birds
armed with scarlet cuss words

superheated

on behalf of the one or the other.

Goldfish

Cutglass waters

        Fingers straining out

                Clasping thoughts—

that scuttle away . . .

        Like silvery coppery goldfish.

A Space of One's Own

In 1929
Virginia Woolf
sitting
in a room of her own
urges women
to occupy a space in the house
as their own
as only then
can women be as productive
as men
entirely
on their own.

Usually
it has only been men
who have colonized spaces in places—
studies, libraries, garages, workrooms,
mancaves, and bro-rooms.

Fortunately
in 2019
women too can claim such places in spaces
or even the house itself
as their right

Cont.

to fight
or not
to create
or not
to vegetate
or not
to be
or not.

Roaring Rain Roaring

Roaring rain, roaring rain
on the metal roofing
dripping lustre
on the old Pihimbiya tree
bare, gaunt branches
swinging at living
interrupted by—

flashes and quivers of lightning
tremors and reels of thunder.

The tight of the clutch
of their bodies—swaddled—
lush velvet in the dusk.

Rain roaring, rain roaring
on the roofing metal
dripping lustre
down the old Pihimbiya bark
fresh emerald saplings
snatching at loving
interrupted by—

bursts and streaks of lightning
quakes and rolls of thunder.

Of the Yala Safari Park

Sun
the constant in magnificence, banishing the dense and the dark

Skies
turning rose, turning copper, turning silver, turning gold

Shrubs
harsh spindly skeletons crouching, receiving, saluting, worshipping

Drought
a haze of rust dust on tracts and tracts of horizon

                              as the wildlife
                         come thundering out
                                in multitudes
                     in their jeeps and jalopies.

Empathy

Only a draught of dread
cramming your gullet
clutching your lungs
evaporating your tongue
flagging your limbs
discharging your bowels
when you hear them come
outside your gate
could perhaps make
you
empathize
with the scapegoats of your hate

but
then again
could it?

If it did
you would not hate

history would not repeat
nor
regurgitate.

The Bracelet

Opal icicles encircling my wrist

stalactites stretching down my elbow

stalagmites twisting my fingers

into talons of ice

as I try to be nice.

Time

Lotus white petals of tomorrow
already surrendering
to the jade buds of yesteryear
blooming expectantly into being.

We cycle perpetually
among the ferns and fronds of today
decapitated
by the prospect of time.

Time and Time

Time and time
he sits
by the table lamp
with his ancient magnifying glass
reading deep damson histories
and pale lilac futures
in the constellations of his palm.

Have the tenses of time merged
in the opaque apse of his mind?
Is he a captive—locked
in the dawning of the past?
In the dusking of the future?
Space becoming time
unrolling
like an endless psychedelic kilim?
Time cycling eternally
over and over again?
Or maybe,
he too, is innate to time?

In any case
time has ceased to tick or tock.

Time Again

Time and time again
tells us:

Be alert
to my temporality

aware that
I am unfolding
unfolding
unfolding

as I am Time

do not
turn to me—
with memories afire
either in churning loss
or in smouldering grief
or curdling desire

come to me
in no other way
than
with the ease of tranquillity.

With an acceptance
of irrevocability.

Identity Politics

These days
we tiptoe,
demi pointe, pirouette,
summersault,
even pole vault
lest
we offend,
and the Opinionators find fault,
and squash us
with a juggernaut.

Blood Relatives

The first time Mia's spouse
was elected
to political leadership,
a relative of fairly remote affinity,
possibly fancying himself
the patriarch
of an extensive political dynasty,
deemed it imperative
to send her an explicit tree
splayed with her blood ancestry

to her utter ignominy.

Arms perched with
aunts and uncles
nieces and nephews
grand aunts and grand uncles
first cousins and second cousins and third cousins
cats, dogs, goats and carbuncles
along with their status, workplace
and qualifications
—information
considered vital
in employment generation
presumably
under her husband's dispensation.

The Course of the Disease

Black blood aflame
like fever

burning with fervour

ignited like wasps
around the shadowy beard of a nest
on a comb of trees
amidst the paddy-green fields.

Raw nerves plucked out of the way
by a conspiracy of ravens
to uncover the inflamed joint
and bare the warped white bone.

The disease quickens its course

swells the sinews tight
stiffens the limbs solid
stains the skin red.

Locks me

with pain that
deadens the living
and enlivens the dead.

Progress

The earth
gashed open
flaming red and raw

for a sightseer's café
on the tea-green
mountainside

(a fetid ulcer
on a youthful
skinned knee)

for the sake
of progress
(or panorama)

with no remorse,
responsibility
(or refuge)

from the landslide
to follow
with the next deluge.

Sea Change

Nightfall at noon

auras of streetlamps
smudges in the gloom

waves of sweeping rain
slating against the windowpane.

Flame trees turgid with water
lurching down
to the ground

all the while
the brute outside roars

to be let in the room.

Offerings

I have roses for you

a bouquet of downy ruby roses
a kaftan of shaded dusky roses
Ms Dior's Eau de Toilette (Rose N'Roses)
lace-edged handkerchiefs of damask roses
a sketchbook of vivid garden roses
a birthday cake of peach cream tea roses

still locked in my gift trunk
two years later

Though perhaps not the birthday cake.

The Majority Men

Sister,
you wonder how to flee—
the palpable possibility
of prowling packs of the Majority men
flaunting swords and sickles
sticks and stones
—without detection.

Sister,
I know,
I will never feel
the acid sear of fear
in your gut
that can never heal—
given past recollections.

Sister,
words forsake me—
at the void between us
at the perfidy of the Majority
men striding the country
with the privilege
—of impunity.

Cont.

Sister,
feel my pulsing heart,
bleeding out
the shame of the tribe
the guilt of the majority
—steeped in demagogy.

A Thought

If we are not our bodies nor our actions
if we are not our minds nor our thoughts
nor our habits nor intentions
then
what are we?

Faculty Meeting

Dear Dean,
would you mind
if we whimper—a little?
We are well aware that
it is not done for us
to growl or howl
in the face of
immense aggravation
for the want of a
rapid-firing machine gun,
especially,
in this illustrious congregation
of eminent scholastic
starfruits, passions, and bananas
holding up their persnickety noses
humbling creative collegiate courses
humping their individual hobbyhorses
hindering away the arable hours
not forgetting
the rows of lemons and oranges
whose zealous wisdom and forages
can never be debunked;
giving the distinctive impression
at every scheduled faculty session
of the precise length, depth, breadth

Cont.

of familiarity
with every single subject—
as we sit pretty
following the death
of our integrity.

After the Taking

And if I am taken

on that day
as it seems these takings happen
not in the black of night
but in the bright of day

in vans that are a rusty white
bespattered with collateral blood
by men who have discarded their uniforms
who have bared their branch-like forearms
who wear frozen coals on their faces
and,
a blood lust on their moustaches.

And if I am taken

during daylight

like those many others before me
who have ended up disappeared,
permanently

should I go with shrieking throat
or mute — with teeth clenched tight?

Cont.

Would I be able to withstand
the drowning by water
the burning by fire
the choking of air
the burial under soil
the days of corporeal torture
in the hours,
leaching . . .
before the black of death?

And if I am taken

on that day
disappeared like many before me
perhaps to reappear . . .
only in subaltern history

Then,
after the delivery of incisive speeches
after the composition of media pieces
after the signature on cyber petitions
after the filing of judicial cases
and,
after the roar of enraged citizens

what else can you do?

Untitled

The swollen, silver sky
hangs . . .
on men with eyes of steel
executing
their selected roles of

Hegemonic Masculinity.

1983[1]

Lying supine
one night
on the shimmering slab
of smooth granite
flanking
the glimmering lagoon,
fainéant with wine,
and the whimsey
of an arpeggio on guitar . . .
Viewing
the northern celestial
hemisphere;
the spectral landscape
incandescent
with molten silvery light
as the speckled opaline platter
ascends . . .
on to the tip
of our adulthood—
with absolutely
no inkling
of the bloody
lunar eclipse
to come.

---

[1] 1983 is considered a turning point in the civil war in Sri Lanka when the Tamil people around the island were persecuted and killed by Sinhala mobs and opportunists as payback for the killing of thirteen soldiers by militants in the north of the country.

Aftermath

The flesh wounds of combat
may have healed
a decade later
but
the throbbing scabs of memory
remain unpeeled as yet
while
underneath
the embers of the soul
smoulder impotently
at night.

Flare-up

Hands frozen
quicksilver
pulsating
in the snarl of blue veins

moulded bronze feet
clenched and calcified

dry grey bones cracking inside.

How do I rupture the black ice
to turn the brass knob
to open the door
to walk out

before I fracture into dust?

Seafaring

Centuries ago
maritime ships
resplendent with ivory sails,
masts, ropes and rigging
steering the Indian Ocean
seafaring from the Temasek
to Arabia and back
bearing the name X-Press Pearl
would contain chests of brocades and silks,
caskets of coffee and tea,
canisters of rice and spice,
pouches of pearls
of lustrous white,
nacreous grey, luminous gold,
perhaps even pearlescent pink,
garnered from the blue.

Centuries later
a nautical vessel
of rust-hued steel
laden with dull containers
sailing from
Singapore to Dubai and back
concealing contagion
would burn and burn and sink

Cont.

secreting
toxin after toxin,
corroding schools of flickering fish,
desiccating shoals of reefs,
slaying grasslands of coast,
leaving behind
sea spans and eons
of annihilation.

Let's Read Poetry

Nowadays,
we prefer to judge
rather than understand,
to answer rather than ask,
observes
Milan Kundera.[2]

Nowadays,
we prefer to text
rather than speak,
write rather than read,
post rather than probe,
perform rather than experience.

Nowadays,
we prefer to pontificate
rather than communicate,
take offence rather than vindicate,
politicize rather than analyse,
protest rather than resolve.

---

[2] Quotation attributed to Milan Kundera in Ruweyda Ahmed, 'To be a writer means to discover a truth': Milan Kundera—a life in quotes' in The Guardian of Wednesday 12 July 2023.

Cont.

Now, let's read for traces, presences, nuances, and absences
let's read for reiterations and valuations; centres and margins,
and errors
let's read for incongruities, certainties, instabilities and
bipolarities
let's read for diversities, relativities, multiplicities, universalities,
and univocities
let's read poetry.

Pteropodidae

Grey shit splattered,
splotched on amber tile roofs,
white parapet walls,
and mildewed stone paving.

For months and months and months,
they heard the
incessant
sandpapery
squealing, squealing, squealing . . .

Downy black tears
poised motionless
on leafless branches
waiting
to drop.

And at times
swooping down
and
soaring up
and
swirling around
marauding the mango tree.

Cont.

Enhancing the season of unease,
excreting disease,
auguring death,
and threatening mortal devastation.

Bats—
can fruit bats truly do that?

Can they truly be a trope of the times?
or
is it all in their minds?

Unkind,
the neighbours are alert and ready
fortified with a cache of fireworks
to subvert their common destiny.

Extinction

This cursed death
that culls the species
of the Anthropocene
as its septic civilizations
scramble for an edge
scouring for
rapid counteractions,
proactive medications,
prized vaccinations,
immunity augmentations,
and herbal distillations;
heeding to
political fatuities,
senseless sorceries,
preposterous ceremonies,
appalling prophesies
and even
pathetic fallacies;
all the while
clawing—
to survive.

This feckless disrespect
for a global consensus
to eradicate the virus
makes it obvious—
even Jean-Jacques Rousseau's

Cont.

original noble savages
and Charles Darwin's
fittest of the fittest
would no doubt
be ultimately
annihilated
by this vulgar virus —
wave by pandemic wave,
mutation by genetic mutation,
body by human body;
phased out
in the toll of death
over the next decade
— perhaps
like the
dinosaur clade?

Für Elise

The deific rapture of Beethoven's *Für Elise*
humbled to a metallic automated tune
pronouncing the arrival of Colombo's *Bread and Banis*[3]
piercing the tranquillity of the afternoon.

---

[3] Tea Bun

The Metaphysics of Lockdown

Action stopped
stifled
suspended . . .

Time prevailed
pervaded
persisted . . .

Space collapsed
condensed
congealed . . .

Place bound
bordered
bolted . . . . .

In stasis,
awaiting . . .

Discovery

It is a perfect marble head
an unyielding glass globule
with endless crystal tints
intriguing to my touch
budding a tactile tadpole tail
as I watch
and return
again and again
to feel this cancer
nascent in my breast.

Karkinos[+]

To run
to fly
to flee
to outrun
your body   —from the grotesque of
                      the Karkinos stirring—   shifting its scab
                                                                lifting its claw
                                                                engorging itself
And   within you.
were it
not possible,

to run
to fly
to flee
to outlive
your body,   then,
                                                to unclothe
                                                to scrape off
                                                to shed
                                                your body

like the hoary skin of a snake
so that the mind can ascend free…

[+] The term cancer originated from the Greek word karkinos, meaning 'crab'.
It was later Latinized as cancer.

Why Not Me?

After the diagnosis
of
a carcinoma in my breast,
a friend appeased me,
why you?

But then it occurred to me,
why not me?
Fairly unappreciated,
my life has vacillated:
from the humble to the sublime,
from the academic to the aesthetic,
from the global to the spiritual,
and to
the mundane and ridiculous;
amidst
the congestion of living.

Back then,
I never inquired
why me?

Cytotoxicity

Forever submerged
in this gentian violet ocean

intermittently plummeting
in currents of chemo

relentlessly tortured
by this howling, gnawing ghoul
in the belly

sometimes drifting
into the depths of opacity

sightless, soundless, and removed
far from reality.

Absence

Of late
I have begun to think
of life
without me

when
for some
there would be
without me
an absence
of presence.

No loud clanking of the front door
no clattering footstep on the stair
no clamorous greeting of care.
No deskbound silhouette in the booth
no typing figure on the laptop
no expounding don at the lectern.

But
for others
there would be
without me
a presence of
absence.

Irascibility

Dearest friends, relatives,
and acquaintances,
much as I love you dearly,
can you please listen to me—
sincerely?

I just want
to vent and vacillate
to rant and rave and rage
to groan and gripe and
basically
bellyache.

I don't want to hear about
your friends' experiences of
fancier cancers
the bloody wankers
or the malignancy of your mister
or the cancerous blister of your sister.

or about the empathetic ache
in your arm or knee or stomach.
How inconsiderate!

I don't want you to urge me
to be positive, pray,

Cont.

exercise, or meditate
to change my fate
as if
I myself have not researched
those activities
to get
a rebate
on life.
I don't want to hear about
your WhatsApp fixer
of ginger, saffron, turmeric, ochre,
and other shades of yellow
as an elixir.

I don't want to hear you
balance my options
calculate my pros and cons,
as though I have become
an inexplicable
docile imbecile.

I certainly don't want
your counsel on cancer—
it's not as if you have
actually had it
or you can find a tonic
or vaccinate it
damn it.

Cont.

Nor do I want you to tell me
your estimation
of the management of
my own destination.
So, without giving me
advice and admonition
as if I caught this disease
through my own volition

can you just simply dry up

and listen?

The Scream

Today
you comprehend
the Norwegian painter
Edward Munch's
unnerving artwork
The Scream

of incomprehensible woe
of resounding painted whirls
from the mouth of an alien skull
contorted into an 'O'.

Because
today
you want to scream . . .

You want to grimace
grind and gnash your teeth
want to open out your mouth
and dislocate your jaws
to pulverize
your throat.

And
scream out your guts
incessantly.

Privilege Political

Shall we
simplify it?
privilege political
some have it
some don't
some misappropriate it
others won't.
societies confer it
and retract it
politicians parade it
capitalists desire it
socialists are sanctimonious
nevertheless
justify it
when they acquire it
and
that seems to be
the sum of it!

Political Strategy

My mind
sits
stiff
swollen
indigo blue
as I watch them
demonize
you

maliciously

misconstructing
something
out of nothing;
deconstructing
everything
into nothing

tenaciously

making untrue
into true;
making true
into untrue

sedulously

Cont.

assembling
wrongs from
hitherto rights;
dissembling
hitherto rights as
wrongs

to
demonize
you.

Losing it

Words—they disappear
as she seeks them
in dim linguistic crevices.

Images—they evaporate
as she seeks them
in obscure optical contours.

Thoughts—they perish
as she seeks them
in spent cerebral chambers.

Memories—they dissolve
as she seeks them
in desolate temporal caverns

within her mind.

Yet

some nameless vistas
still remain
in the boiling tar-black
of her consciousness.

Cont.

But still, she hunts
her mind's meshwork
for them that hide . . .

Soothing herself
with profundity . . .
awaiting
the return of
normality . . .
discounting
any other
probability.

Ambiguity

Feet planted on either side
I straddle
the taut pawns
of political opinion
on a black-and-white checkerboard
so steadfast
in outrage and certitude.

I squat
feet straining against
the incessant push
of political pigeonholing
despite
the tones of grey
in each ideological standpoint.

Who can stand upright
against
these incensed irrationals,
against the ruddy feet of centipedes
speeding to feed on us
in these times of
piercing ethical ambiguity?[5]

---

[5] A couple of days after this poem was written in 2022 (during the country's economic/political crisis), the house of the poet and her spouse was burnt down—purportedly by political protestors.

Politicizing the Personal

On several days
they came
they stood
they chanted
a personal catechism
outside our home
upright
righteous
and
apparently
'peaceful'
always precedes
these protesters
who activated
their cause of
politicizing the personal.

No
they were not
propelled by Machiavellian strategy
not
motivated by memes or media,
or images or imaginings,
nor inflamed by insinuation,
or enraged by rumour,
or even routed by rancour.

Cont.

No
they did not
cart their sacks of odium,
nor bray the brine of abhorrence,
or even spew the acid of spite.

And no
most certainly not—
they did not
lug the load of fuel
to spray the home from top to bottom
from inside out
to strike the stick that lit the blitz
and no
did not free the water
from the hydrant
nor bar the fire brigade
from coming through
to douse the blaze l'orange

to personalize the political.

Flamingo Red

Flamingo red
our home
lit up the Colombo sky
as it burned and burned
in my imagination
while others watched it live

paragraphs, words, letters
on pages curling up in flames,
tufts of scorched paper,
scraps of sepia photos
floating off
into the inky night
devoured by passers by

signs, symbols, souvenirs
of life lived
loves cherished
legacies received
losses accepted
maladies endured

a sanctuary,
no, a sanctum
taken for granted

Cont.

now violated and erased
incinerated as memory.

The civilization of a nation
interrupted repeatedly
by frenzies of violence
histories of hate
ravages of loss
vestiges of grief

our own
othered, maligned,
obliterated,
regularly

reduced to savour
the aftertaste of ashes
of acid ideopolitical clashes.

What remains then is
the liberation of choice

to be defined
defiled
defeated
by the futile feats
of putrid hatred

or
to take refuge
in the grace of intellect.

Random Culpability

I guess it's quite natural
these days,
to see a random man or woman
walking down the road,
and lapse
into wondering:

Were you one of them?

That night,
were you one of them
that invaded our home

amidst the flood of mindless bodies
(the imagery of seething, surging activists)
amidst the swarm of roaring hornets
(the allusion uttered by a wounded driver
quailing for his life)
amidst the rash of random ragers
(the alliteration echoing in my mind
with dramatic effect)

self-mandated to enact
an act
what you may justify as
a rational hate,

Cont.

an incited passion
or was it instead
a dead cold stratagem?

Either which way
let it matter not
to me.

For
if I seek you out
uncover your name, body, face,
then, I too become culpable
of what I see as
the irrationality
of hate.

Sanctuary—A Flash Poem

Our home. A sanctuary. No longer.

Cinders at the tips of my fingers.

Shadow

I must say that it's been a while
perhaps even a lifespan
since I have seen her
yet
always
she has been there
watching me, miming me,
waiting uncomplainingly
and perhaps very soon
I would be watching her
miming her, shadowing her,
morphing uncomplainingly
together with
the sky, the stars, and the sea
into the mystery of infinity.

Sunbreak on Silver

Sunbreak
over the Malacca Straits
within reach of
gravid grey clouds bursting
to show burnished silver and iridium fire
within.

Pewter smudges of ships
on the slatey seas of silvery scales
far below.

Gliding through the smoky silver haze
of
iridescence
stretching into the stratosphere.

Ethereal splendour
that promise
of serenity,
of love,
of bliss.

Amma's Advice

Fifty years later
Amma's advice to me
still resounds
in me . . .

If ever your husband
or any other madman
(for that matter)
ventures to strike you
'for whatever purpose'
just because
he feels he can,

be ready—

do not permit yourself
to be surprised,
or traumatized;
do not shrivel in shame,
or prickle with pride,
or feel scandalized;

do not be a martyr—

but inhale into your lungs
the breath of outrage

Cont.

and
rage . . . rage . . . rage . . .

rage out
aloud

bring down the house
bring in the neighbours
bring out the forces

bring about a speedy
close
to your vestal hopes

do not forget—

we must
take umbrage at men's atrocities;
articulate wrath
at our battered histories;
and ultimately
carve, contour and create
our emancipatory trajectories.

Cont.

Recollection

My father's radio room
was a festoon of junk

under a mounted *Amateur Radio Map of the World*
a panel of hand-built wireless sets (now vintage)
of aluminium and steel transmitters, receivers,
and a vast transformer
with curious knobs, switches and dials
(though home-made)
were tremendously sophisticated for the age

counters of transistor apparatus,
hand tools and equipment
amateur radio microphones and Rediffusion speakers
1960s and 70s adapters and antiquated meters
old copper valve radios and wireless moderators
miniature acres of electronic circuit boards and breakers

jam bottles of bolts and nails and rivets and pivots
on open cupboards and shelves with neat labels
pails of scrap iron and hardware instruments
black spiral wires, multi-coloured filaments
stretches of flexes and strands of copper cables

stacks and racks of QSL cards personalized,
printed and posted

Cont.

with the call sign of each Radio Ham
from Austria to Zambia
from the Arctic north to the south of the Antarctica
from eastmost Fiji to westmost Kiribati,
and unfamiliar regions such as Corsica and Cambria.

My father's radio room
was a cacophony of sound

when tuning and turning the dial
for Amateur Radio Hams
an eccentric orchestra across the scale
of the 40-meter band
of steady humming and occasional murmuring
to high-pitched squealing
of chitter and chatter, jibber and jabber,
of babble and gabble
of peeps and beeps, and the tooting and tapping
of Morse Code by hand

My father's usually mild voice acquires
a sturdy and velvety burr
when hailing other Ham Radio amateurs

'Calling CQ CQ CQ Calling CQ
This is 4S7SW
4S7 Sugar Whiskey
Calling CQ CQ CQ'

Cont.

Unexpectedly

Unexpectedly,

the reach of your arm—in silence
the touch of your hand—a question
the press of mine—in response
the trace of your finger pads—insistent
the caress of my thumb—in replay
the scratch of your fingernail—a prelude
the resistance from mine—scarcely
the forage of my forefinger—furtively
the crush of your grasp—urgently

the closing of our hands
the clasping of our fingers
the clenching of our palms.

Unexpectedly...

The Last

Last —

you gazed up at me
long
intent
inscrutable

seated
in your customary seat
on your customary side
of the automobile

just before you left.

I did not come to you
though I knew
your eyes beckoned me
to —

did not know
that it would be
for the
last—
only happens
in retrospect.

The Coming of Death

Always the hands-on handyman around the house
my Thaththa
while puncturing the whitewashed wall
with an electric drill
was felled to the ground
like a colossal tree stump.

My feet are heavy — like boulders . . . .
were his last words.

Before
my uncle from next door
placed Thaththa's weighty feet on his own,
enfolded him around the waist
(Thaththa's head slumped on uncle's shoulder
deep furrows dragging down his ashen cheeks)
stalled, swayed, staggered him to the bed
a waltz of the grotesque . . .
before
the rattle of death of breath.

The panic to resuscitate
perhaps some hot Horlicks?

He's not responding
turn him

Cont.

Left? Right? On his back
Pump his chest
One—Two—Three—
Push - up — to — thirty

Mouth-to-mouth
breath propelling breath.

Scraps of first-aid training
Girl Guides?
The Fire Service Department?
St John's Ambulance?
now called upon as first respondents.

Years later
I realize that he had been dying
feet first.

Afterwards,
my mother's words,
raw, forever seared—
black rhombi on the pink mush of my brain
like chargrilled salmon.

Cont.

Ceased to Be

Sometime in the starless depths of

Wednesday morning

my mother ceased to be

my mother

ceased

to be.

Can Dying Be Done Tonight?

Can dying be done
like a haute cuisine,
fusion dinner in sequence,
each dish designed as a serendipitous surprise

chilled melon balls in champagne,
coconut-battered shrimp with spicy marmalade,
chilli tamarind sorbet,
lemongrass crab,
whiskey tres leches and
espresso with salted caramelized nuts,

degustation
in dim candlelight.

Perhaps dying can be done
like a public birthday bash
a free-for-all —
with anyone and everyone embraced

Battenberg cake,
button mutton cutlets,
pepper-eyed egg boats,
bright-coloured vegetable pinwheels,
waning spring rolls with MD tomato sauce,
syrupy iced coffee and
free-flowing alcohol,

Cont.

loud revelry
in open daylight.

Dying can certainly be done
under callous public consumption
without any interventions
of comfort, duty or humanity

The decapitated head
of a beloved mother
in the clasp of a daughter
crazed with grief
(severed by
the wheel of a motor lorry)
ignominiously seized on camera,
posted and passed on social media—
feasted ferociously for private gratification

on a main street
in the dead of an urban afternoon.

Yet, for all
dying is done
alone

In irrational fear,
in rational evaluation,
in embodied distress,
in struggling consciousness,

Cont.

in the coldness of limb,
in the stiffness of bone,
in the crushing weight of chest,
panting with puerile panic—
until the mind and body
can synchronize the acceptance of

dying in a whisper
tonight.

Dying Dispassionately

With reassuring conviction
Osho[6] offers an insight on dying:

If you can
at the juncture of death
when you are left
with no further sentience

telescope and microscope
your focus

concurrently

to channel the touch of your mind
onto the cusp of your nostril
on to the wisp and waft and wane of your breath
literally
on to the still of presence.

If you can
periscope yourself
from the motion of living

---

[6] Known under many aliases, Osho was considered a controversial new Indian
religious leader.

Cont.

sublimate your consciousness
to observe formally
the kaleidoscope of passions
of awareness, of attachment, of agitation,
of agony
at the impending expiry
of life.

Apparently,
you can then
seize the moment of dying
and witness yourself
die
dispassionately.

Never Again

Let me recognize
the boundaries of Time
and work within
rather than against
the ontological frames
that constrain me.

Let me acquaint my mind
to the acceptance of never.

Never to see
never to hear
never to be
never to know
never to return.

Never
again.

A Perfect Death

Thinking a few random thoughts
planning to rise at 6 a.m.
revise a chapter on feminist ethics
Sashimi with Roshi
Ah, the sheerness of the lush cotton sheets
and then
the heaviness of sleep

dozing off then
deeper and deeper
and losing myself

forever

without knowing

that I will never awaken
again

ever

unaware

that it has been
a perfect death.

Beyond

My mind
keeps expanding
infinitesimally
through unfathomable fathoms.
I pass by a squillion of stars
to the deadness beyond.
Or do they
pass me by?

Now receding
into the obscurity of space
to unite
with the vacuum of time
to sever
from the pulse of life
within the metaphysics of
my mind.

The Remains

Once gone
is it possible
for there to remain
a trace of a scent
a trace of a sight
a trace of a sound
a trace of a taste
a trace of a touch
a trace of an aura
perhaps in some
other forma
that can be found
by sniffer dogs?

Afterthought

I wonder whether it is pretentious
nowadays
to inscribe one's thoughts
in rainbow arches,
in darkening gulches,
in archaic cultures
of poetry?

No doubt writing them in prose
can make for
an eclectic readership, higher visibility,
perhaps even fame, fortune and validity.

Nonetheless,
the pristine precision,
perhaps even
intuitive vision
of a poem
—despite its compression
and abstraction—
cannot be attained by the exigence
of prose,
which usually calls for a surfeit of words.

Part Two

In Extremis
(March 2020–July 2022)

'In Extremis was written during the stretch of time when the
Sri Lankan nation was battling the polycrisis of the Covid
pandemic, economic free fall, climate change, political revolts
and other existential transformations, and while the poet was
mitigating life-threatening illness.'

In Extremis
(March 2020–July 2022)

I

I used to think
that we lived in
an age of
neoliberal excess,
but that was
before this
existential regress,
this stress—
this distress—
of a malevolent virus,
of a political thiasus,
of an economic hiatus,
of a climatic problematic,
of a carcinogenic cyst,
culminating in this
post-postmodern extremis
if one can call it—this.

I mean, for us
the privileged
of our genus,
there was an endless
abundance of
callous consumption,
or so we thought.

Cont.

Now
during this soundless night,
during this cessation of life,
during this epoch of pestilence,
I hear the basso bellowing of the ocean
and my abdomen quakes and quivers
when I think of the quicksands
of the times to come.

For the past
has spent itself—
expired,
unable to become
the future,
unable to repent or repeat
the cycle of time,
unable to offer
even a tender green
shoot of hope
for this age of forfeiture.

Our adversary,
that sloped the scale,
is an
indiscernible germ
that glides in the air,
that strikes us unaware,
sans forewarning
of disease and demise,
leaving

Cont.

our bodies locked
in ascetic extremis . . .

We are stranded

within the fault lines
of our fundamental premise,
within a serrated split in paradigm,
of what we consider to be
the truths of our realities
that have rapidly gone amiss . . .
with the gilded fantasies
of the two last centuries
democracy / modernization
decaying into debris
in our hands.

While the steel grey of today
sags
interrupted
by sparkles of soft
champagne sunshine . . .
the much-awaited monsoon
splutters to arrive
amidst spurts and squalls,
but the Kachchan[7] winds
shall blow and blow and blow

---

[7] A hot, dry, west or southwest wind or foehn that blows during the southwest monsoon in June and July.

Cont.

within the lee of
the south-western hills.

Government gazette
upon gazette upon gazette
extraordinaire
of the monocratic state
of the inconsistent autocrat,
of the kleptocratic state
of the patriotic bandits,
of the stratocratic state
of the arbitrary military,
of the theocratic state
of the raucous monks,
of the oligarchic state
of the licensed sycophants,
of the technocratic state
of the pseudo-professionals,

govern us now...

'Our rage spills crimson
upon these tarred roads
but then
will revolt alone be enough?'

Thirsting for the truth . . .
The truth or any truth:
searching, researching,
quantifying, qualifying,

Cont.

collaborating, confabulating,
constructing, deconstructing,
reconstructing, dismembering,
googling, opining, truth-tabling,
experimenting, replicating, predicating,
validating, meditating,
praying

for a truth
ceaselessly . . .

Meanwhile, I,
I sit bald, bald, bald,
a naked, wasted gecko,
my browless eyes
beholding the world
in sheer extremis,
while other
browless geckos
observe me
audaciously.

II
Dropping down
at dusk,
one by one by one,
the white velvet Araliya[8]
tinged celestial gold,

---

[8] The Frangipani flower associated with worship in Buddhist temples

Cont.

its sacred fragrance
tangled, mangled
by the sandalled feet
of the saffron priests
as there are no barefoot
clerics in the 21st century.

The acute lenses
of CCTV cams and drones
observe us,
doggedly,
with minuscule eyes,
as we run
hither and thither

or dither

and play the zither,
or the xylophone,
or the trombone,
each to be different
from one another . . .

to be different
from the sameness,
to be different,
to be different,
to
be
dif—fe—rent . . .

Cont.

Long after the spirit
has departed,
Big Pharma Barracudas
continue to withhold,
and watch you,
pledged, wedged,
to the machines and
apparatus of healing care,
of oxygen, nutrition,
waste and wear,
rasping for breath,
gasping for death . . .

'Manike Mage Hithe
Hithe Mage Manike'[9]

While we women
have been induced
under lockdown
to grind and grind
and grind ourselves into grits
for household production,
for sexual reproduction,
until one day,
a woman's palm
squashed the blood-sucking
silver-black, striped, parasite
within her family.

---

[9] A rephrased refrain from a popular song that went viral during the period

Cont.

'What's the score, Machang[10]?
What's the score?
questions the old Royalist
from the older Thomian[11].'

Does the responsibility lie
with the gory brothers
of the Southern Tribe
who have slaughtered
the truth,
rolled it up in a reed mat,
incinerated it,
buried its ashes in the backyard
and grown organic vegetables
and sunflowers on its graveyard?

This heat
this intolerable heat,
that saps us dry
into the husks of our lives,
while we hear the naked infants
bawling
for release . . .
show me a future
other than in a mirage
of an aircraft

---

[10] Term of camaraderie
[11] Reference to the score of a historical cricket match between two renowned boys' schools in Colombo

Cont.

radiating
on the tarmac
about to depart
yet, it offers no relief

but an aberration of
your hope.

'And still
the dead keep dying . . .
in extremis,
forsaken,
in the desolation
of isolation.'

While others perform and post
and mediatize their lives
in endless self-revelation,
in the sameness of brunch,
in the sameness of brand,
in the sameness of backdrop,
rebelling
with insentient uniformity . . .

this insentient uniformity
in difference,
this uniformity,
this uniformity,
this
u—ni—for—mi—ty . . .

Cont.

The eyes of these potato potentates
cannot see
that in Amparai, in Kurunegala,
the variegated greenscapes
of paddy
will soon lie fallow,
hill upon hill upon hill
of the dark tea-green leaves
will wilt and wither into flakes,
while the flaxen shoots of corn
and the rotund red tomatoes
will be devoured
by writhing maggots and spotted fungi,
due to their half-baked agrarian policy.

'Human Rights, if you speak,
if you are Muslim or Tamil,
if you speak, Human Rights,
they will efface you, like Hejaaz[12],
for months and months and months,
or forever
like all those others,
just because
we brothers can.'

Should we then
leave a garland
of ivy greens

―――――――――
[12] A Sri Lankan lawyer and human rights defender

Cont.

and arum lilies
to mourn the
demise of Truth,
who is survived by
a posy of reactivist opinions
spun on the web
and scattered by
an array of media dominions.

'Will everyone, someone, anyone
take responsibility for this
Gotterdammerung?[13]'

III
Sans volition,
we are
photographed and posted
surveilled and identified,
our data
filed and algorithmized,
predicted and projected
(not only by Netflix);
we are, therefore,
the numericized objects,
the digitalized subjects,
of the
looming Totalitarian State,

---

[13] A situation of world-altering devastation marked by extreme chaos and violence.

Cont.

of leeching Global Tech,
of relentless Kapital Das.

A man of white cloth
with the chilli red sash
(not to be confused with
a *kurakkan*[14] shawl),
is righteous in his unrighteous anger
unrighteous in his righteous anger.

Ayioo!
these digital influencers,
exactly who are these masses
that they reach?
asks Aunty Mabel affectedly;
can they reach out
and give a hand
to that single mother, Seelawathi,
starving and sweltering
in the Kalu Gal Quarry?[15]

'I keep telling you—
it's not the cancer
that is killing me,
it's the chemo . . .'

If it were
ontologically possible

---

[14] Millet coloured
[15] Granite

Cont.

to be that categorical,
then, certainly
though contestably,
the human condition is
a postmodern one,
or perhaps
even post-postmodern,
when all is said and done,
and, apparently,
all has been said before,
if not, done.

Oh, to be clever, clever, clever!

'Of course,
the smartest of all
might well be
the humble mobile phone.'

Blemishes on the sun,
followed by
days and days of shadow,
followed by
crashing rain
falling on
burnt-orange soil crumbling under your feet,
land sliding off hilltops and highlands,
falling on
creeks, cascades, canals,
rivers, swamplands,

Cont.

overflowing on
hamlets and households,
suburbs and settlements,
townships and the metropolis . . .

portending the gloaming years
of the Kali Yuga.[16]

You!
yes, you,
reading this discursive spiel
you who advocate these vain men
and vacuous manifestos,
constitutional amendments
and system changes,
opposition unity and
a third political force,
or even an intergenerational revolution;
when perhaps,
it's you and I
who need to alter and sacrifice.

'Do we look forward
and repeat the cycles of history
or do we look back
to rupture them in futurity?'

---

[16] In Hinduism, it is the fourth and final epoch of the world cycle before it is destroyed to be recreated once again. It is considered to be an age of extremes, conflicts and sin.

Cont.

A speck of spittle
spews from
Kamla's mouth
inadvertently;
the fire ants insist
on calling her out,
in phony offence;
furiously—
fretting, feeding,
fighting, fuming
over this little word
in digital space;
utterly unforgiving
of accidents and errors;
predators with malintent,
trolling her,
evoking nocturnal terrors.

Some think that the answer lies
in political determination
in the red-hot, raw, and radical?
in the square, sedate, and seasoned?
in the moderate, balanced, and blended?
or should we look for a
totally fresh ontological solution?

In the Sinhala Buddhist bowl
of the land
their minds are burning, burning,
burning

Cont.

like a funeral pyre,
its scarlet glow
gyrating higher and higher.

But these days
we can only grasp
at the possibilities
of truths
(in the plural);
no accuracy, no authority,
no certainty, no consistency,
no integrity, no legitimacy.

'And we continue to ask 69[17] of them—
would they hunt the golden lion
and eat his barbequed flesh
during the famine to come?'

And do I still think that
liberal democracy
will save me?
Even centuries ago,
the Athenians knew
that She was just
a perverted myth—
whether direct,
or representative,
or otherwise,

---

[17] 69 lakh people who voted for President Gothabhaya Rajapakse

Cont.

but today
even She is gunned down
by post-postmodern practice.

'So why are we ready to
believe the
conspiracy theories behind
every bush and thicket?'

And then,
our turn will come,
our forlorn bodies
will be trussed
in plastic and cardboard,
vacuum-sealed
like Norwegian smoked salmon,
and shunted into the furnace
before becoming
shades of mauve
and shadows of mulberry
in the evening sky
without rite[18] or
adequate reason.

'Mindless, mindless,
mindlessness of being
as opposed to the mindful,

---

[18] During the early stages of the pandemic, Muslim people who died from Covid 19 were denied burial rites and their bodies were cremated.

Cont.

mindful, mindfulness of being—
is this intrinsic bipolarity
another religious epistemology?'

IV
And still
the Northern woman
Sivaranjani
stands still—
by the roadside,
in Mullaitivu,
a hand on her hip,
the sun on her head,
a glint in her nostril,
awaiting
the arrival
of Transitional Justice
by the SLTB bus . . .
but He never comes,
meanwhile
lifetimes have passed
in the limpid eyes
of the Thamil Sahodhari[19]
even though she is only
threescore years of age.

'Of course, the truth
may never be known.'

---

[19] Sister in Tamil

Cont.

But all hail the new truths
of the era:
affronts, intrigues, inanities, litanies,
banalities, home truths, homilies,
totalities, fatalities, celebrities,
fake news, memes, remedies,
parodies, indiscriminate generalities.

While others say that
enraged generations
of woke
though awoken to virtue
have gone
West by West
without an address . . .

The unending glare of
Monday, Tuesday,
Wednesday . . .
turn to days
turn to weeks
turn to months
its dense yellow underbelly
dank and bloated
hunkers over Colombo . . .
smothers
the pitiless lines of pitiless people

awaiting . . .

Cont.

Once you hear it—
recapped again
and again and again,
once you see it—
posted again
and again and again
not only by the Ministry of
Public Enlightenment
but by the motley civets
of public activism—
don't worry,
it becomes the truth.

I watch . . .
the ageless vine
scaling our balcony,
wildly,
its lime-green leaves
arid to the touch,
like sandpaper,
its bone-coloured stems
gnarled and grasping,
like skeletal fingers;
yet, the violet sprigs of
the queen's wreath
have not bloomed
for many decades;
still—
it keeps me nourished
during these months

Cont.

of consuming cancer,
showing me life
as I have never seen before.

One law for all,
another law for others,
all laws for one,
no laws for some,
and then, finally,
will you be done
or will it all come
undone?

In extremis then:
our existences,
our actualities,
our practicalities,
our inevitabilities,
our veracities,
our realities.

Foreshadowing
the tropic of anarchy
we echo
the Red Offshoots:

'Burn them, burn them,
burn them out—
the 225.'[20]

---

[20]   225 members of the Sri Lankan Parliament

Cont.

Of course,
they are not you or I
and certainly not you or RW,
don't get me wrong—
they are not Muslims or Tamils
this new other that we now hate,
and can justifiably blame
and castrate.

How or when, then,
will the rage of this age
abate?

Yet on reflection,
can we definitively blame or absolve?
can we truly reason who or why or how?
can we actually trace cause or effect
or action or reaction

to
the politicization of religion
the religionization of commodities
the commodification of products
the production of technology
the technologization of industry
the industrialization of the globe
the globalization of multinationals
the multi-nationalization of capitalism
the capitalization of democracy
the democratization of the digital

Cont.

the digitalization of politics
the politicization of religion . . .

While our religious dignitaries pronounce:

Sadhu Sadhu Sadhu
Aaamen Inshalla
Om Shanthi Shanthi Shanthi

'As you can see,
ultimately,
there is no sense
in the common
nor any commonality
in sense,
only a growing consensus
for utter tendentious nonsense'.

You keep telling me
you want hope, hope, hope
please give me Hope . . .

So
was it remiss
of me to think
that there was
Hope in the proverbial East?

In the East
is that Hope we see

Cont.

is that Hope we
is that Hope
is that
not

Perhaps
from these throes of nihilism,
the aged, disparaged, sage—
Ayesha
can salvage
some pearls of iridescence
that could transcend our existence.

Even then,
eventually,

our Time will skulk off
to the naked acreages
of the Sinharaja;[21]
to heave and heave and heave,
birthing in extremis—
yet another premise
of a thesis, antithesis, synthesis,
or another bloodstained
cosmic metamorphosis,
or perhaps a butterfly fluttering
to materialize from a chrysalis,

---

[21] A rainforest in Sri Lanka

Cont.

all of which,
will not shackle us,

as finally
we will be free

yet mercifully,
not there
to see.

Scan QR code to access the
Penguin Random House India website